You Might Be Addicted to Mah Jongg If...

You have room for only one carry on, and you choose your Mah Jongg bag!

A Humorous Collection of Mah Jongg Creations

Mary Anne Puleio, Ph.D.

A **Smile Üp** Book

Published by Smile Up, LLC

Special Edition Contains Original Art in Full Color

ISBN 978-0-9907211-3-0

ATTENTION CORPORATIONS, EDUCATIONAL INSTITUTIONS, ORGANIZATIONS and TEACHERS:
Quantity discounts are available of this book for educational or gift purchases.
Special books or book excerpts can also be created by the author to fit specific needs. For
information, please contact Smile Up, LLC, 3991 Gulf Shore Blvd. North, #301, Naples, FL 34103;
(239) 248-3578 or visit the Smile Up, LLC website at: www.smileup.org.

Inspiration

Having had a successful and demanding career in the Information Industry, stress had taken its toll on me. I was exhausted. As a diversion, a dear friend, Cathy Wooster, taught me to play Mah Jongg. Skeptical that I would really get it, I devoured whatever books I could find on the subject. Faster to learn than bridge and more challenging than cards, I was hooked. With perseverance, I became proficient. I even began teaching the game. Eventually, I have been able to bring many people together, at all levels, to play.

Mah Jongg is fun, social and for me a true blessing. My joy from the game began to inspire my creative side. One day, I started sketching a tile with a personality — this is how BAMS was born. Soon all the tiles had morphed into characters from my imagination. Simultaneously, I saw a need for an easy and fun guide that would combine the technical side of Mah Jongg with humor. I knew this would make it more accessible and less intimidating to learn. This is when, *How to Play Mah Jongg: The Quick and Easy Guide to the American Game*, emerged and has been a true success.

The benefits of playing Mah Jongg go far beyond the game. I am most grateful for the friendships and laughter. Perhaps, you can also relate to this? So, here's wishing you much joy, and of course many smiles looking at this humorous side of Mah Jongg.

The Players: BAMS, CRAKS and DOTS.

What you love most about Springtime is the arrival
of your new official Mah Jongg playing card!

You keep thinking about previous cards...
Well I always felt unwanted, but things really went
South when they took NEWS off the playing card!

You love Mah Jongg themed celebrations!

You Might Be Addicted to Mah Jongg If...

© Mary Anne Buleis

MAH JONGG

Not even an incredible fear of water, will keep you from the annual Mah Jongg cruise!

You don't go anywhere without a Mah Jongg
bag in your trunk.

You enjoy yummy Mah Jongg treats!

Sunny Mah Jongg thoughts make you smile!

You Might Be Addicted to Mah Jongg If...

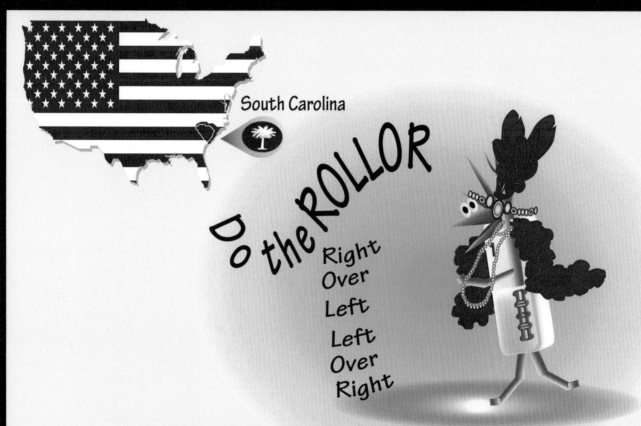

South Carolina

Do the ROLLOR

Right
Over

Left

Left
Over
Right

© Mary Anne Pulsio

The Mah Jongg Charleston

The first thing that comes to you when hearing Charleston is no longer a city in South Carolina!

You start adding: "When playing Mah Jongg" to the end of your fortune cookie messages!

If you could, you would play
Mah Jongg every day of the week!

You always have room for one more
Mah Jongg accessory!

You know exactly what hand some friends will play.

© Mary Anne Bulcis

You daydream about finding a pot of gold!

You secretly search for more challenging players.

You seek game advice but, the reading was apparently a hoax, when a joker was used in a pair!

You appreciate the perfect gift,
"How thoughtful, fresh Jokers!"

You're always looking for new players...
"It's great Kitty dragged in a sub, but I think she's having trouble focusing on the game!"

You appreciate a little Mah Jongg support!

All you really want for the holidays is more Jokers!

You're always planting new Mah Jongg seeds.

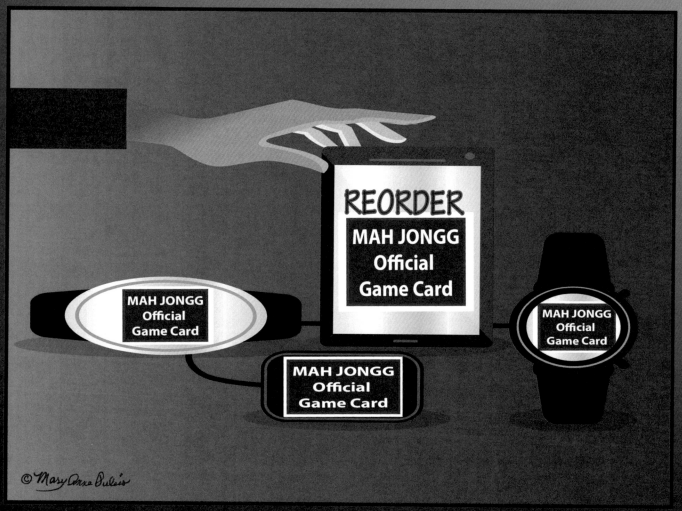

You synchronize all your smart devices to alert you to the exact moment to reorder the new Mah Jongg card!

Thinking about Mah Jongg calms your nerves
during stressful encounters!

You appreciate no tricks, just Mah Jongg treats!

You become suspicious of some players.

It's time to celebrate
when you break your losing streak!

You start waiting for your "Tiles to Speak to You" before deciding what hand to play!

You tolerate annoying players.

You know some cool Mah Jongg chicks!

Some players test your patience,
but you play with them anyway!

You keep seeing Jokers in your meditation.

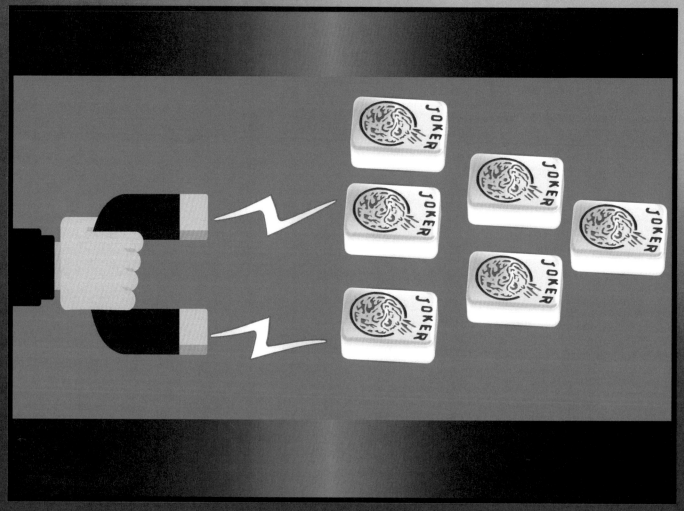

You secretly magnetize the Jokers to come to you.

Accused of not racking loud enough, you take extreme measures. Can you hear me rack now?!

You imagine seeing Jokers everywhere!

You love sharing Mah Jongg treats —
Take One!

When the coast is clear, you slip out
of events to catch a Mah Jongg game!

You know Joker Vultures will quickly appear
when the hand is declared dead.

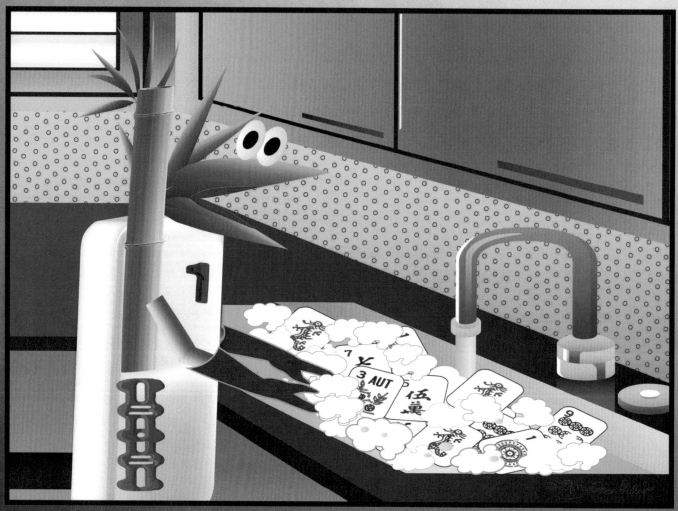

Accused of not having squeaky clean tiles —
you wash each one by hand.

Still not clean enough, you resort to using the dishwasher to get squeaky clean tiles!

You carefully dry each of your now—
squeaky clean tiles!

You start counting Jokers to fall asleep.

You're always searching for new Mah Jongg players.

Win or lose, you're always
grateful to play Mah Jongg!

You're shocked to commit a fatal error — picking a discarded tile while playing a concealed hand!

Spread the gift.
Teach someone to play Mah Jongg.

I wish you much joy and happiness playing this wonderful game.
If you have a fun Mah Jongg story or experience to share,
please contact me at: smileup.org
It may become the next humorous illustration!

Also Available:

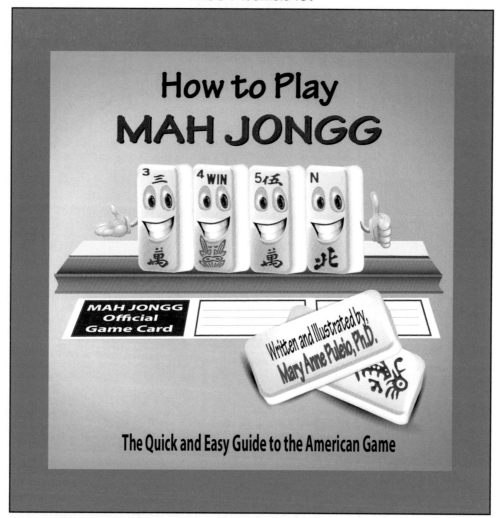

How to Play
MAH JONGG

MAH JONGG
Official
Game Card

Written and Illustrated by,
Mary Anne Puleio, Ph.D.

The Quick and Easy Guide to the American Game

- **Presented in an easy-to-learn format**
- **Illustrated in full color with original art which helps you to understand and remember key points**
- **An excellent take-along guide for quick reference**
- **A great teacher's manual for beginners**

"Original and easy to understand, this guide will have you smiling and quickly playing Mah Jongg."

Also Available:

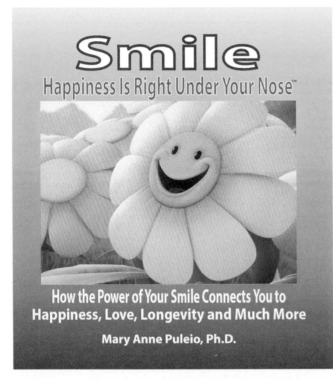

Smile
Happiness Is Right Under Your Nose™

How the Power of Your Smile Connects You to
Happiness, Love, Longevity and Much More

Mary Anne Puleio, Ph.D.

Most of us are under utilizing the incredible power of our smile.

Now the author has deciphered hundreds of current scientific studies on the smile, and presents it in a unique format that is easy and entertaining to read. The findings will astound you, and instantly motivate you to tap into the remarkable power of your smile to:

• **LIVE LONGER**: Frequent smilers add seven years to their life span.

• **BE HEALTHIER**: Smile and your body produces powerful hormones that decrease pain, accelerate healing, and improve mood.

• **RAISE SELF-ESTEEM**: Share your sincere smile and people are more likely to judge you as confident and beautiful.

Compelling and profound, you will want to share this book with everyone that is important to you!

"Travels, producing and speaking engagements can wear me down, but my sails were filled instantly by your thought provoking book."
Scott Hamilton, Olympic Gold Medalist & Best-Selling Author

"This book is terrific. I want all my kids to read it!"
Toni Dovolani, Dance Pro on America's *Dancing with the Stars*

"This book helps remind me of the confidence and joy I gained in my life from making others smile."
Florence Henderson, Legendary Broadway, Film & TV Star

Mary Anne Puleio is an award-winning professional speaker, author and artist. Proceeds from the sale of her books are designated to assist nonprofit organizations helping children born with facial deformities. For additional information, or to see her original creations, or to share information visit: **www.smileup.org**

Made in the USA
Lexington, KY
27 March 2019